The JOY of COLOURING BY NUMBERS

Illustrated by Felicity French and Lauren Farnsworth
Cover design by Angie Allison and Jade Moore
Designed by Jade Moore
Edited by Zoe Clark

Complete the 25 stunning pictures in this book by following
the number codes to reveal a vibrant palette on every page.

Don't worry if you don't have pens or pencils that exactly match the
colour key. Darker colours can be achieved by applying more pressure
with a pencil and lighter ones by pressing gently. With pens, you can
layer ink to achieve different shades. You can also create new, unique
colours by blending two shades together. In some pictures you will
notice blank areas without numbers inside. These should be left white.

There are finished versions of the pictures at the back of the book,
just in case you can't wait to find out what they look like.

It's time to relax, get creative and bring these
images to life with gorgeous colour.

Michael O'Mara Books Limited

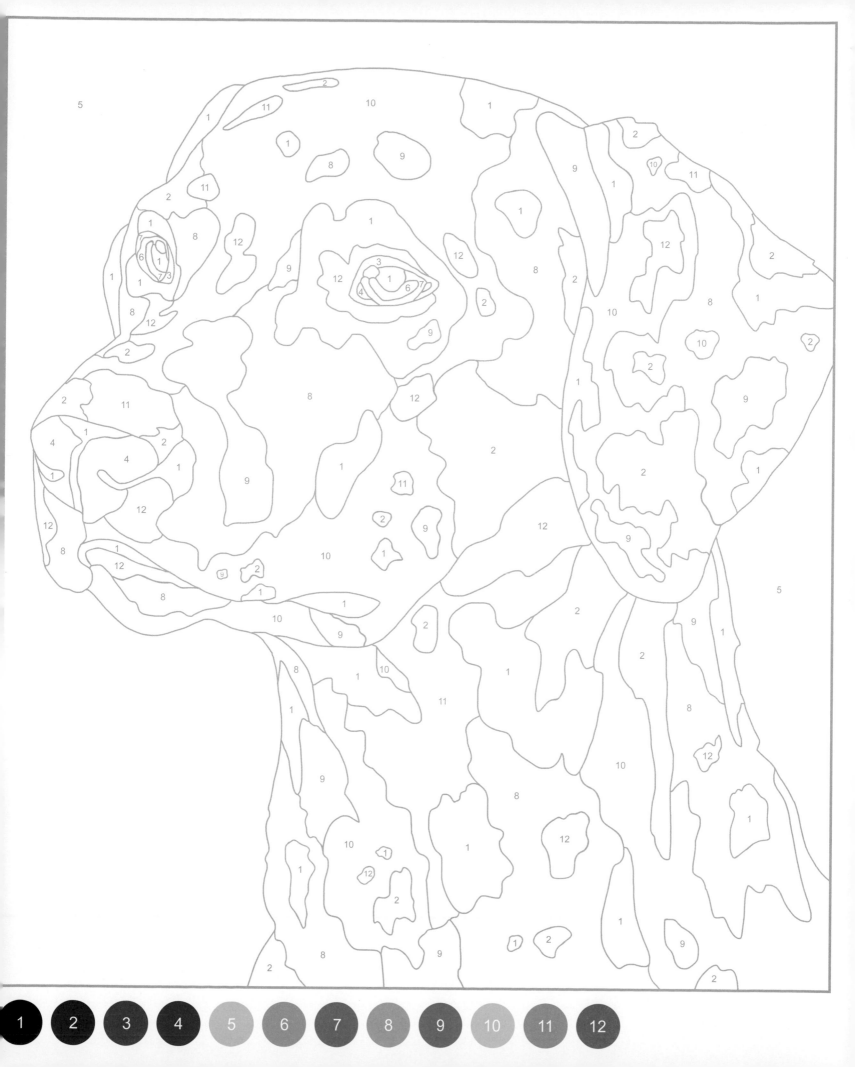

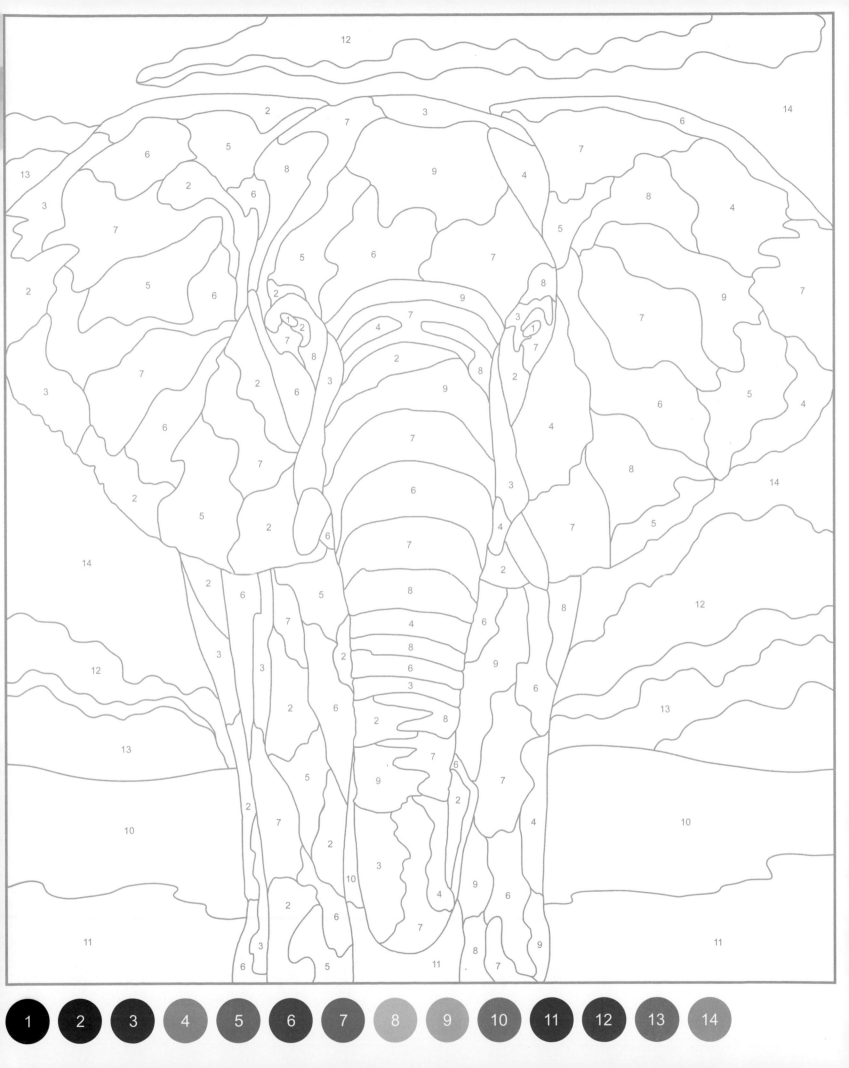

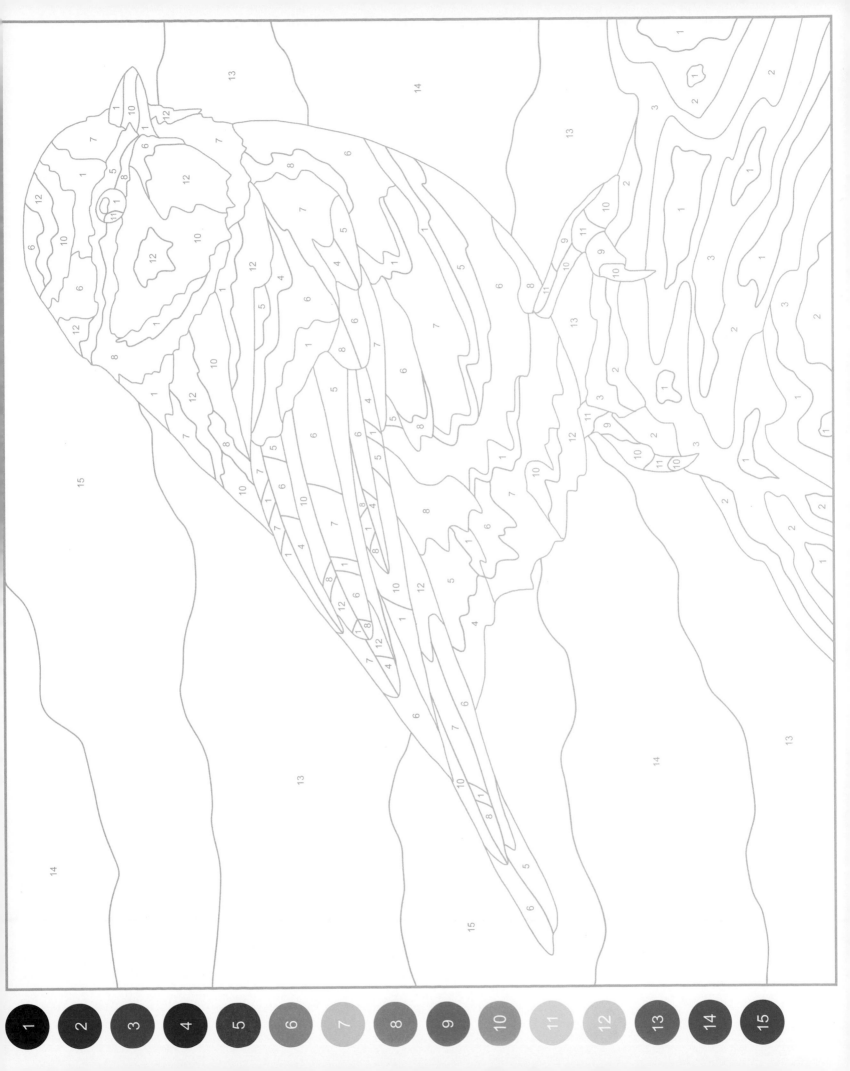

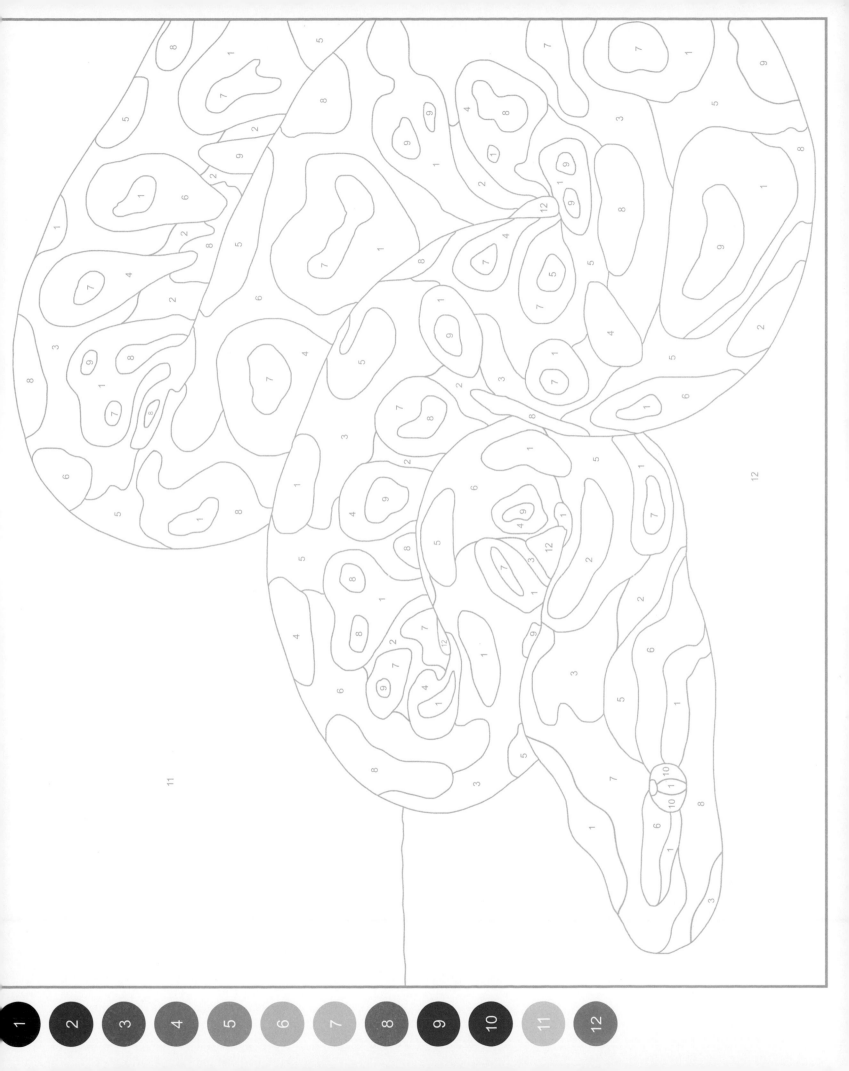

First published in Great Britain in 2023 by Michael O'Mara Books Limited,
9 Lion Yard, Tremadoc Road, London SW4 7NQ

W www.mombooks.com   f Michael O'Mara Books   🐦 @OMaraBooks   📷 @omarabooks

The material in this book was previously published in
Patternation: A Tangle-By-Numbers Challenge.

Copyright © Michael O'Mara Books Limited 2017, 2023

A CIP catalogue record for this book is available from the British Library.

ISBN: 978-1-78929-503-0

1 3 5 7 9 10 8 6 4 2

This book was printed in China.